Hills of Fuzz

by Tamera Williams
illustrated by Kersti Frigell

Core Decodable 32

McGraw Hill Education

Bothell, WA • Chicago, IL • Columbus, OH • New York, NY

MHEonline.com

Send all inquiries to:
McGraw-Hill Education
8787 Orion Place
Columbus, OH 43240

ISBN: 978-0-02-144863-0
MHID: 0-02-144863-9

Printed in Canada.

9 10 11 12 KOD 24

Zack zigzags past Liz.

As he zags, bits of fuzz drop.

Zack hums as he zigs and zags.

As he hums, lots of fuzz drops.

Zack stops.

He stands in hills of fuzz.

"Is he still a bug?" asks Liz.

"I am Zack," he grins.